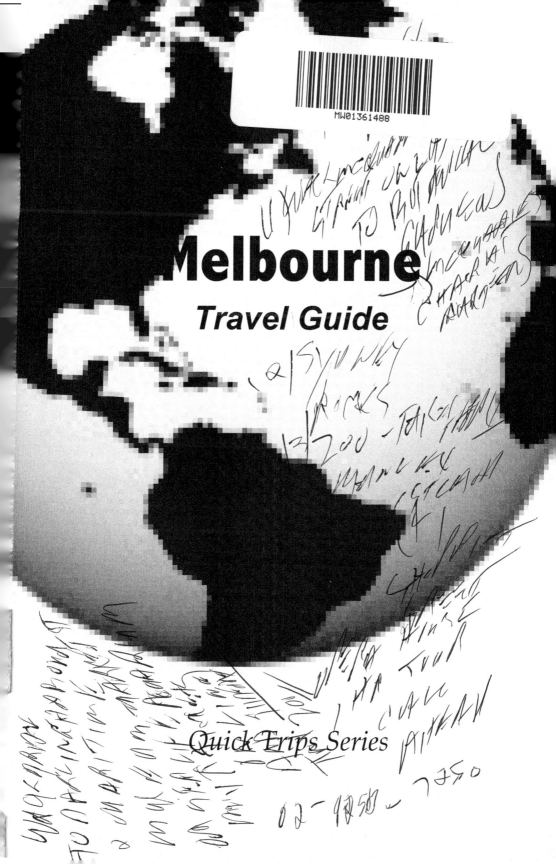

Melbourne
Travel Guide

Quick Trips Series

No part of this publication may be reproduced, stored in a retrieval system, or transmitted, in any form or by any means without the prior written permission of the publisher, nor be otherwise circulated in any form of binding or cover other than that in which it is published and without similar condition being imposed on the subsequent purchaser. If there are any errors or omissions in copyright acknowledgements the publisher will be pleased to insert the appropriate acknowledgement in any subsequent printing of this publication. Although we have taken all reasonable care in researching this book we make no warranty about the accuracy or completeness of its content and disclaim all liability arising from its use.

Copyright © 2016, Astute Press
All Rights Reserved.

Table of Contents

MELBOURNE — 6

- CUSTOMS & CULTURE 8
- WEATHER & BEST TIME TO VISIT 9
- GEOGRAPHY 9
  - City Centre 10
  - Southbank 11
  - St. Kilda 11
  - South Melbourne 12
  - Carlton 12
  - Fitzroy 13

SIGHTS & ACTIVITIES: WHAT TO SEE & DO — 14

- FEDERATION SQUARE 14
- AUSTRALIAN CENTRE FOR THE MOVING IMAGE (ACMI) 16
- ROYAL BOTANIC GARDENS MELBOURNE 17
- NATIONAL GALLERY OF VICTORIA 19
  - NGV International 20
  - The Ian Potter Centre 21
- EUREKA SKYDECK 88 21
- MELBOURNE ZOO 23
- OLD MELBOURNE GAOL (JAIL) 24
- SCIENCEWORKS 26

The Lightning Room 26
  Melbourne Planetarium 27
  House Secrets 27
  Sportsworks 27
  Explore-a-saurus 27
  Transportation 28
  Opening Hours 28
- **BEACHES** **28**
  St. Kilda Beach 29
  Brighton Beach 29
  Port Melbourne, South Melbourne & Middle Park 30
  Kerford Road Beach 30
  Elwood & Williamstown Beaches 30
- **MELBOURNE CITY TOURIST SHUTTLE** **31**

BUDGET TIPS 33

- **ACCOMMODATION** **33**
  Hotel Claremont Guest House 34
  Greenhouse Backpackers 35
  Habitat HQ 36
  Melbourne Central YHA 37
  Melbourne Metro YHA 38
- **RESTAURANTS, CAFÉS & BARS** **39**
  Andrew's Hamburgers 40
  The Beach Albert Park 41
  A Minor Place 42
  39 Pizzeria & Degustation Bar 43
  Bar Lourinha 44
- **SHOPPING** **45**

Smith Street, Collingwood..46
Bridge Road, Richmond 46
Queen Victoria Market 47
Melbourne Central 48
Bourke Street, CBD 50

KNOW BEFORE YOU GO   52

🌐 Entry Requirements 52

🌐 Health Insurance 52

🌐 Travelling with Pets 53

🌐 Airports 55

🌐 Airlines 57

🌐 Hubs 59

🌐 Money Matters 59

🌐 Currency 59

🌐 Banking/ATMs 60

🌐 Credit Cards 60

🌐 Tourist Tax 61

🌐 Claiming Back VAT 61

🌐 Tipping Policy 62

🌐 Connectivity 63

    Mobile Phones 63

🌐 Dialling Code 64

🌐 Emergency Numbers 64

🌐 General Information 64

🌐 Public Holidays 64

🌐 Time Zones 65

🌐 Daylight Savings Time...66

- School Holidays 66
- Trading Hours 67
- Driving Policy 67
- Drinking Policy 68
- Smoking Policy 69
- Electricity 69
- Food & Drink 70
- Useful Websites 72

MELBOURNE TRAVEL GUIDE

Melbourne

Melbourne is Australia's second largest city and the capital of the state of Victoria. The city is often mentioned as Australia's finest and offers numerous galleries, parks,

MELBOURNE TRAVEL GUIDE

museums and theatres alongside beaches, cafes and shopping. Many people use the city as a base from which to explore the surrounding areas of the **Great Ocean Road** and the **Grampians National Park.**

About one million visitors come to the city every year. Walk through the several acres of parkland or take a break in the plentiful restaurants and bars. Visit the oldest building in Melbourne, the **Mitre Tavern**, which was built in the year 1837 or take a ride to the top of the tallest building, **Eureka Tower.**

Melbourne welcomes all with its city centre nature, its culture and its beauty. City heritage controls on the heights of buildings make Melbourne attractive-looking while highlighting its architecture. Melbourne has well-

MELBOURNE TRAVEL GUIDE

maintained gardens and features fine art and science museums. There is a free tourist bus service and some of the best sights are free. Melbourne is a nature lover's city. It offers paths for walking and bicycling at the beaches along with hotels which are often equipped with eco-friendly features.

🌏 Customs & Culture

Melbourne is one of the cultural centres of Australia and has Victorian architecture, theatres, parks, gardens, galleries and museums. The four million residents of the city are big fans of sports and cultural events. The city boasts an active live music scene and an impressive food and coffee culture. The people here tend to dress up more as the climate is more changeable and cooler than in Sydney.

MELBOURNE TRAVEL GUIDE

Particularly important events in Melbourne include the **International Film Festival** which is held every August and the **Comedy Festival** which is held in April. The **International Art Festival** is held in October. There are many museums including those dedicated to immigration, science, banking, sports, film, railways and Chinese History.

🌏 Weather & Best Time to Visit

The weather of Melbourne is often described as having "four seasons in a day" with lots of springtime and autumnal-type weather. The city receives about 24 inches of rainfall each year and the wettest month is usually October. An average summer day in Melbourne has a temperature of around 79-86° F (26-30° C). The inland

MELBOURNE TRAVEL GUIDE

suburbs tend to be hotter than the coastal areas which enjoy a refreshing southerly breeze. Daytime temperatures in summer can exceed 104 °F (40 °C) and heatwaves are quite common.

🌏 Geography

Melbourne is located in southeastern Australia and is surrounded by the Dandenong mountain range, the Yarra River and the Mornington Peninsula.

The population of the city is made up of people from all walks of life and Melbourne is a multi-cultural and affluent city with a several sub-communities. The city is home to people with their origins in countries like Italy and Greece (Melbourne has the largest Greek population outside of Greece) as well as other communities including Arabic,

MELBOURNE TRAVEL GUIDE

Muslim, Vietnamese, Latvian, Indian, Chinese, Portuguese, Spanish, Serbian and African.

City Centre

This is the business district of Melbourne and is the historical core built on the Yarra River. The area includes the newly developed region of Docklands towards the west. This district is the site of some big developments like the NGV arts precinct, shopping malls and buildings of historical importance. The most impressive feature in the city centre is Federation Square, which incorporates galleries, atriums, bars, cinemas, cafes, restaurants and business centres.

MELBOURNE TRAVEL GUIDE

Southbank

This region is the hub of fine dining, the fabulous Crown Casino and is offers much to keep the tourist entertained.

It is located 1 km away from the central business district on the southbank of the Yarra River. The area features many striking high-rise buildings. The Victorian Arts Centre is one of the big attractions has somewhat resembles the Eiffel Tower of Paris. Other attractions include the Melbourne Convention Centre and the Aquarium. There is also a large number of restaurants, shops and cafes located here.

St. Kilda

St. Kilda offers great beaches and a vibrant nightlife. It is located to the south of the city centre and is close to Port

MELBOURNE TRAVEL GUIDE

Philip Bay. The largest tourist attractions include the beaches of St. Kilda and Elwood, St. Kilda pier, Botanical Gardens and Marina. The district also houses the historic amusement area of Lune Park and the beachfront area known as the Esplanade.

South Melbourne

South Melbourne consists of the old ports of the city as well as the town centre and the historically important Clarendon Street. South Melbourne is also home to the Royal Botanic Gardens and the Southgate leisure and shopping development. Also look for the famous Melbourne Cricket Ground (MCG) and the excellent restaurant district in and near Clarendon Street.

MELBOURNE TRAVEL GUIDE

Carlton

This is the University district and is also famous for its cuisine. Lygon Street features a large number of shops, cafes and pizzerias and draws food and coffee lovers from all parts.

There is a wide range of stores visit. The Melbourne Zoo, the Royal Exhibition Building and the Melbourne Museum are also located in this district.

Fitzroy

Fitzroy, the smallest district of Melbourne, is unique due to its small lanes and narrow streets. One way streets are also common here, making driving more complicated. The entertainment centre of Fitzroy is Brunswick Street, which is a major eating, entertainment and shopping area in

MELBOURNE TRAVEL GUIDE

Melbourne. The nearby Gertrude and Smith Streets are also well known for their great cafes and vintage stores.

MELBOURNE TRAVEL GUIDE

Sights & Activities: What to See & Do

🌏 Federation Square

Corner Swanston & Flinders St

Melbourne

Victoria 3000

+ 613 9655 1900

http://www.fedsquare.com/

MELBOURNE TRAVEL GUIDE

Federation Square is one of the largest free attractions of Melbourne.

It comprises an entire block of the city and is the work of Australian architects Bates Smart in association with Lab Architecture. It offers a unique combination of cultural and civic activities and has been recognized all over the world as one of the great public spaces.

Federation Square plays host to more than 2000 events every year. The square is always buzzing with exhibitions, performances, events, festivals, concerts, forums and fashion shows. The square is most conveniently located opposite the Flinders Street Station in the city centre (also an iconic Melbourne sight).

MELBOURNE TRAVEL GUIDE

Australian Centre for the Moving Image (ACMI)

Corner Swanston & Flinders St

Melbourne

Victoria 3000

+61 (03) 8663 2200

http://www.acmi.net.au/

Immerse yourself in the world of television, digital culture and film at the Australian Centre for the Moving Image. It is home to the popular film festivals of Melbourne and special programs for kids and seniors as well as showing classic movies. ACMI hosts a free exhibition known as **Screen Worlds** along with hosting international and Australian cinema.

MELBOURNE TRAVEL GUIDE

Visit the largest screen gallery in the world to see the exhibition or watch films in any of the auditoriums or hear from leading film and TV personalities. A ticket for a movie costs around $15.

There is a bar/café overlooking the Federation Square and the ACMI store which offers interesting merchandise for movie buffs.

Catch a train to the Flinders Street Station to reach the ACMI. You can also catch a tram to Flinders Street Station. The ACMI is open everyday from 10 am to 6 pm. It is closed on 25th December.

MELBOURNE TRAVEL GUIDE

🌐 Royal Botanic Gardens Melbourne

Birdwood Ave

South Yarra

Victoria 3141

+61 – 03 9252 2300

http://www.rbg.vic.gov.au/

The Royal Botanic Gardens of Melbourne is a free attraction of the city and attracts over 1.6 million visitors a year. The gardens are a place of delight and discovery and feature a stunning collection of plants and peaceful lakes.

The garden is home to plant collections like succulents, roses, camellias, herbs, cycads, Chinese Plants,

MELBOURNE TRAVEL GUIDE

...an plants, rainforest flora, cacti and perennials. The **Guilfoyle's Volcano** is a newly launched precinct for visitors. The garden also acts as a sanctuary for wildlife including eels, black swans, cockatoos, kookaburras and bell birds.

The **Ian Potter Foundation Children's Garden** is a popular attraction for children. The garden has everything a child could ever want. It features crawling tunnels, a forest in which to play hide-and-seek and it rocks for climbing.

The garden hosts tours and walks for visitors wanting to learn about the cultural significance and the history of the garden. Tours start from the Observatory Gate meeting point. After enjoying the beauty of the garden take a break at the Observatory Café or the Terrace Tearooms.

MELBOURNE TRAVEL GUIDE

You can take a tram (numbers 5, 8, 16 or 67) from Flinders Street Station and get off at Domain Junction to reach the Royal Botanic Gardens.

The Royal Botanic Gardens are open everyday from 7:30 am to 8:30 pm. The Ian Potter Foundation Children's Garden is open through Wednesdays to Sundays from 10 am to 4 pm. It is closed during the school holidays of July.

🌐 National Gallery of Victoria

180 St Kilda Rd

Melbourne

Victoria 3004

+03 8662 1555 (10am-5pm)

http://www.ngv.vic.gov.au/

MELBOURNE TRAVEL GUIDE

The National Gallery of Victoria consists of two galleries located at a short distance from each other and both of them are free to enter. The NGV stretches from St Kilda Road to the Federation Square and consists of the NGV International, the Arts Centre and the Ian Potter Centre all located a short walk from one another.

NGV International

180 St. Kilda Road, Melbourne

NGV displays the best of Asian, European, American and Oceanic Art. Since the time the gallery was opened in the year 1968, the collection has almost doubled. The building is one of the most iconic in Melbourne and the

MELBOURNE TRAVEL GUIDE

gallery has been revamped to house one of the most significant collections of the world.

The Ian Potter Centre

NGV Australia at Federation Square

The Ian Potter Centre is home to art of Australian origin from the present to colonial times. There is more Australian art on display here than in any other gallery in the world. The Ian Potter Centre also features a restaurant and a café.

Take tram numbers 1, 5, 6, 22, 64 or 72 from St Kilda Road/Swanston Street and get off at the Victorian Arts Centre Stop. You can also take a train to Flinders Street Station and walk from there. The NGV International is

MELBOURNE TRAVEL GUIDE

open from Wednesday to Monday from 10 am to 5 pm and remains closed on Tuesdays.

🌐 Eureka Skydeck 88

7 Riverside Quay

Southbank, Victoria 3006

+03 9693 8888

http://www.eurekaskydeck.com.au/

$18.50 (Adult)

$14 (Concession)

There is nothing to prepare you for the sight from the top of highest building in Australia, the Eureka Tower. It is a must-visit for visitors to Melbourne. The two elevators take you to the top of the building in less than a minute and then you are propelled to the **Edge**, a sliding cube made of glass (with the visitors inside!)

In addition to the unparalleled view, the Eureka building will keep you entertained with other interesting activities. You can visit the wall displays, experience the 6 metre Table of Knowledge or simply enjoy taking breathtaking pictures from the terrace.

The Eureka Skydeck 88 is open throughout the year from 10 am to 10 pm and is 5 minutes from Flinders Street Station. Just cross the bridge over the river to get there.

🌐 Melbourne Zoo

Elliott Ave

Parkville, Victoria 3052

MELBOURNE TRAVEL GUIDE

+1300 966 784

http://www.zoo.org.au/melbourne

$26.10 (Adults)

$20.20 (Concession)

Melbourne Zoo is home to more than 250 species of animals from all over the world. The beautiful landscape of the zoo adds to the large variety of the animals located there. Walk around the African and Asian rainforests settings of the zoo to see the monkeys swinging from the trees and the tigers roaming. Stop to watch the orangutans performing their antics or explore the kangaroos, koalas, wombats or platypus and the other unique animals in an Australian bush setting. One of the most recent additions to the zoo is the Wild Sea which displays the penguins of Victoria, the Fur Seals of

MELBOURNE TRAVEL GUIDE

Australia and other animals which are native to the land. There is also a special enclosure for baboons which opened in 2011 and acts as the home to Hamadryas Baboons.

Melbourne Zoo is located at the city centre near Royal Park and can be easily reached by taking Tram 55 or by taking a train to the Royal Park Station from Flinders Street Station.

The zoo is open from 9 am to 5 pm everyday.

Old Melbourne Gaol (Jail)

377 Russell St (between La Trobe St and Victoria St)

+61 3 8663 7228

http://www.oldmelbournegaol.com.au

MELBOURNE TRAVEL GUIDE

$23 (Adult)

$18 (Concession)

The Old Melbourne Gaol is the jail that was used to hold some of Melbourne's criminals in the 19th century (including the famous Ned Kelly). When the jail was built in the 1800's, it used to dominate the skyline of Melbourne. Some of the most dangerous criminals were held inside the jail along with homeless people, petty offenders and the mentally ill. The jail witnessed as many as 133 executions between the years of 1842 and 1929, when it was closed down.

Today the old Melbourne Gaol can be visited to see how its inhabitants were treated back then. The tour of the jail is mostly self-guided and consists of a visit to the cells

MELBOURNE TRAVEL GUIDE

along with film shows. The bones and face mask of Ned Kelly are on display.

Take Tram 24 to stop number 7 or tram 30 to La Trobe Street. You can also take a train to Melbourne Central Station and walk a few minutes to reach the jail.

The Old Melbourne Gaol is open everyday from 9:30 am to 5 pm and is closed on Good Friday and Christmas day.

Scienceworks

2 Booker St

Spotswood, Victoria 3015

+1300 130 152 (9 am to 5 pm)

http://museumvictoria.com.au/scienceworks/

$10.00 (Adults)

MELBOURNE TRAVEL GUIDE

With a wide range of scientific displays and exhibitions on offer, Scienceworks will keep you entertained for hours. You can be a part of the informative tours or experience the live demonstrations. Let us take a look at all that Scienceworks has to offer:

The Lightning Room

The Lightning room gives you a hands-on experience about how lightning is formed and what happens when it strikes the earth. Discover all of this by watching a live show (30 minutes) which is both entertaining and informative.

MELBOURNE TRAVEL GUIDE

Melbourne Planetarium

The Melbourne Planetarium takes you closer to the stars as you recline in your seat to watch some of the most stunning live scenes from outer space.

House Secrets

Explore the scientific facts behind everything you have at your home, from your washing machine to the food that you put in your mouth at the House Secrets.

Sportsworks

Sportsworks features 20 sporting challenges to help you to discover your sporting talents and body profile.

MELBOURNE TRAVEL GUIDE

Explore-a-saurus

Explore-a-saurus is one of the newest additions to Scienceworks and you can discover everything about dinosaurs here. Here you will see comparisons of the types of plants they ate to the recreation of the sound they used to make.

Transportation

Take a train from Williamstown and Werribee line and get down at the Spotswood station. Scienceworks is located at just a distance of 10 minutes from there.

Opening Hours

Scienceworks is open everyday from 10 am to 4:30 pm and is closed on Good Friday and Christmas Day.

 Beaches

Many beaches in Melbourne are watched over by lifesavers during the summer months, public holidays and school holidays.

St. Kilda Beach

St. Kilda is one of the most popular beaches of Melbourne and is great for swimming and other water activities. The St. Kilda Pier is good for viewing the skyline of the city and also for watching the sunset in the evening. There is regular ferry service to Southbank and Williamstown and the marina also offers boating facilities. The area near to the beach has facilities for barbecues and picnic tables. There are also paths for walking, rollerblading and bicycling.

MELBOURNE TRAVEL GUIDE

Brighton Beach

This long stretch of sandy beaches includes Middle Brighton, Dendy Street and Brighton beaches. The region is well known for the colorful huts at the beach-edge. There are also great facilities for playing and barbecuing. Other options include yachting, windsurfing and boating. There are also paths for cycling and walking.

Port Melbourne, South Melbourne & Middle Park

These three beaches are close to the central part of Melbourne and are beautifully wide and sandy. They include paths for bicycling and walking as well as playgrounds. The Middle Park Beach is very popular for activities like beach volleyball and kitesurfing.

MELBOURNE TRAVEL GUIDE

Kerford Road Beach

Kerford Road is very popular beach and has zones to exclude power skiing, sail boarding and boating so offer more protection for swimmers. There are also paths for cycling and walking along with a playground.

Elwood & Williamstown Beaches

These beaches are great for sailing, boating and swimming. There are also boat ramps and cycling and walking paths located nearby along with reserves for play, picnic and barbecue.

Melbourne City Tourist Shuttle

Corner of Flinders & Swanston streets

Melbourne, Victoria 3000

MELBOURNE TRAVEL GUIDE

9658 9658

www.thatsmelbourne.com.au/gettingaroundthecity/visitorassistance/pages/touristshuttle.aspx

The Melbourne City Tourist Shuttle is a service that is free for visitors to the city.

The bus stops at thirteen tourist attractions in the city and you have the option of getting on or off at any of the stops. The 13 stops include Federation Square, Chinatown Precinct, University of Melbourne, Arts Precinct, Lygon Street Precinct, Sports Precinct, Melbourne Museum, Queen Victoria Market, Southbank and Yarra River, Etihad Stadium, Victoria Harbor, Docklands, Waterfront City, Docklands, William Street, The Shrine and the Royal Botanic Gardens.

MELBOURNE TRAVEL GUIDE

The free bus service runs daily from 9:30 am 4:30 pm every 30 minutes. There is no service on Good Friday and Christmas Day.

MELBOURNE TRAVEL GUIDE

Budget Tips

🌏 Accommodation

Melbourne provides accommodation options for every type of budget. It doesn't matter whether you are looking for a backpackers hostel or a luxury hotel; there is no dearth of accommodation in the city. Let us take a look at some recommended places to stay.

MELBOURNE TRAVEL GUIDE

Hotel Claremont Guest House

189 Toorak Rd

South Yarra

Victoria 3141

+03 9826 8000

www.hotelclaremont.com

$60 - $ 149 per night

Hotel Claremont Guest House is unique in offering budget accommodation whilst being located in a multi-million dollar property It is a 77-room Victorian style guest house especially catering to budget travelers. Spend less on your resting place and more on sightseeing and shopping by staying here!

MELBOURNE TRAVEL GUIDE

The guest house offers a 24 hour reception, 77 large, bright rooms, free WIFI, book exchange, internet café, telephone, a pharmacy on the premises, television in all the rooms, guest lounge and complimentary coffee and tea. All towels and bed linen are provided by the hotel and the rooms are serviced once a week. Breakfast is included in your room rate and consists of toast, fruit, cereals, coffee, tea and fruit juice.

Greenhouse Backpackers

Level 6, 228 Flinders Lane

Melbourne, Victoria 3000

+03 9639 6400

Toll Free: 1800 249 207

www.greenhousebackpacker.com.au

MELBOURNE TRAVEL GUIDE

$32 - $35 per night (Dorms)

$80 - $90 per night (Private Rooms)

The Greenhouse Backpackers is located in Flinders Lane and is close to the entertainment district and shopping spots of Melbourne. The hostel boasts of a helpful and friendly staff along with clean and discounted dorms and private rooms to all the guests. Other facilities offered by the hostel include a Mega-Melbourne Walking Tour on Mondays, free WIFI, daily breakfast of cereals, toast, milk, tea or coffee. They offer free pancakes on Sundays at 11 am, a free dinner on Tuesday nights (Australian Barbecue or Pasta) and a big English breakfast on Thursdays.

MELBOURNE TRAVEL GUIDE

Habitat HQ

333 St Kilda Rd

St Kilda, Melbourne

Victoria 3182

+ 03 9537 3777

Toll Free - 1800 202 500

www.habitathq.com.au

$28-$144 per night

Habitat HQ has been recognized as the best budget accommodation in Victoria. It is located in St Kilda and provides more than just a comfortable sleeping experience. The hostel is close to cafes, restaurants and bars as well as to the beaches of St Kilda. The hostel offers various other facilities like free daily music events,

MELBOURNE TRAVEL GUIDE

free WIFI, free breakfast, free keyboard and music guitars for use and free pick-up from the airport!

The hostel also offers free parking and is well known for its love of music. You can rent DVD's and watch them in the comfort of your room and don't miss the terrace view of the sunset. There is a huge guest lounge where you can hang out beside a cozy fireplace. The facilities offered are great and rooms are clean. There is an herb garden and an outdoor courtyard to relax in.

Melbourne Central YHA

562 Flinders Street

Melbourne, Victoria 3000

+613 9621 2523

http://www3.yha.com.au/Hostels/VIC/Melbourne-

MELBOURNE TRAVEL GUIDE

Hostels/Melbourne-Central-Hostel/

$30-$105 per night

This is where you should stay to be close to many of the tourist attractions in Melbourne.

The Melbourne Central YHA Hostel is located in Flinders Street and is very close to the Yarra River and Federation Square. It makes for a quiet bustling stay and provides a good alternative to the rather quiet stays offered by some of the other hotels nearby. The facilities include lounges on all floors, kitchens, high speed internet access and flat screen televisions. There is also a large rooftop deck and daily food and drink specialties. Some other facilities include a bar, a café, a food store and a 24 hour reception.

MELBOURNE TRAVEL GUIDE

Melbourne Metro YHA

78 Howard Street

North Melbourne, Victoria 3051

+ 61 3 9329 8599

http://www3.yha.com.au/Hostels/VIC/Melbourne-Hostels/Melbourne-Metro-Hostel/

$30-$105 per night

Melbourne Metro YHA is located in North Melbourne and offers a panoramic view of the city from its rooftop BBQ and lounge. The hostel features electronic thermostats, solar hot water and an extensive recycling program. It has been accredited by the eco-tourism board of Australia.

The hostel also includes an ATM, Skype, WIFI, bicycle hire and a café. You can enjoy free events and activities,

MELBOURNE TRAVEL GUIDE

free DVD rental, electronic door locks and 24 hour access to the hotel. Some other facilities include a reading room, barbeque, video, television and parking.

🌐 Restaurants, Cafés & Bars

Melbourne is a multi-cultural city and this is reflected in the plethora of cafes, restaurants and bars in the city. The eclectic dining scene has something from every corner of the world. There are some popular dishes which are found everywhere as well as others which you may have never eaten before. Here are a few good choices:

Andrew's Hamburgers

144 Bridport St

Albert Park, Victoria 03206

http://www.andrewshamburgers.com.au/

MELBOURNE TRAVEL GUIDE

Less than $15 per meal

Andrew's Hamburgers is a small café where there are usually five cooks working in a kitchen that is no bigger than the hallway of a house. Spend some time watching them work as they (usually) manage to do everything smoothly and without bumping into each other!

The most popular burger on their menu is "beef burger with the lot" which means ground beef, tomato, bacon, egg, a bun and mayonnaise served with tomato sauce for $9.50.

Andrew's Hamburgers remains crowded pretty much all the time so prepare to wait half an hour for your food.

MELBOURNE TRAVEL GUIDE

Lunchtime is from 11:30 am to 2:30 pm and dinner is from 5 pm to 9 pm.

The Beach Albert Park

97 Beaconsfield Parade

Albert Park, Victoria 3206

+61 3 9690 4642

http://thebeachalbertpark.com.au/

$16.00 - $25 (main course) $7.50 (desserts)

As the name suggests, The Beach Albert Park offers some great food along with a magnificent view of the beach. You can sit with a drink and quietly watch the waves hitting the shore. The restaurant offers both indoor and outdoor dining we'd recommend the latter.

MELBOURNE TRAVEL GUIDE

The beach changes from a laid back eatery to a busy night spot. There is enough space for everybody and you will often find groups chatting the night away. The designer chairs and couches are something to see. The bar opens onto the beach with a beautiful courtyard. A meal for two with a glass of wine will come to about $29 each. The restaurant also offers pizzas and specialty meals for kids. The Beach Albert Park remains open daily from 10 am until late.

A Minor Place

103 Albion Street

Brunswick, Victoria 3056

+61 3 9384 3131

http://www.aminorplace.com.au/

$6.50-$14

MELBOURNE TRAVEL GUIDE

A Minor Place has a large following because of its all day breakfast and Atomica coffee. It is tucked away in a corner in Brunswick, a suburb of Melbourne.

It is everything that a corner café should be. The hot favorites of A Minor Place include toasties, wraps and pides (Turkish bread). The signature dish is Henry's White Beans which is served with toast and dukkah (Egyptian spice mix). The bread served here is organic and the coffee is a special Atomica Blend. The desserts include delicacies like Lemon Tart, Vanilla Cupcakes, Vegan Muffins and Carrot cake. The Minor Place is open through Mondays to Saturdays from 8 am to 5 pm and on Sundays from 8:30 am to 4 pm.

39 Pizzeria & Degustation Bar

362 Little Bourke Street

Melbourne, Victoria 3000

+61 3 9642 0440

http://www.plus39.com.au/

$10 - $22 (Lunch) $10 - $22 (Dinner)

39 is a bar, pizzeria and restaurant with a distinct focus on Italian flavors. It is a simple place that combines the modern and the rustic and can accommodate only a small number of people at any one time. It is a great place for both lunch and breakfast and it offers tasty piadinas (Italian flatbread) with combinations like goats cheese and a selected variety of pizzas at just $10. Other popular options include the lobster and caviar pizza and the fresh Italian salumi (Italian cured meat) and cheeses. The latter

MELBOURNE TRAVEL GUIDE

can be used for complementing your pizza or as a meal in itself. Lunchtime dishes start at $12 and main courses for dinner time starts at $18. 39 Pizzeria and Degustation Bar is open everyday from 7 am to 10:30 pm.

Bar Lourinha

37 Little Collins St

Melbourne, Victoria 3000

(03) 96637890

http://www.barlourinha.com.au/

$24-$35 (Entrée and Main)

Bar Lourinha is an stylish bar which almost looks like a temple. The bar menu features a long list of exotic wines which make perfectly compliment the small plates which come for as little as $12. The bar offers cocktails like

MELBOURNE TRAVEL GUIDE

Montenegro, Punch di Fiamma, Mint and Lemon and Watermelon. There are also Spanish, Japanese and Italian wines available at the bar.

The tapas (small plates) served at the bar are changed according to the day of the week and the season. Some of the best dishes being Paella (Spanish rice) on Wednesday and Lamb on Mondays. Remember to book ahead because the bar is crowded at most times of the day. It is closed on Sunday's.

🌐 Shopping

Melbourne has huge shopping malls like the Melbourne Central as well as many small shops hidden away in quaint alleyways. If there is anything you ever wanted to buy, chances are that you will find it in Melbourne. A must

MELBOURNE TRAVEL GUIDE

visit for any shopaholic is the shopping triangle of the city between the Melbourne Central, the Queen Victoria Market and the Melbourne GPO. Following are some of the best shopping spots in Melbourne:

Smith Street, Collingwood

Smith Street

Fitzroy, Melbourne, Victoria 306

http://www.smithstreet.org.au/

Smith Street is the place to go for buying leisure, outdoor and sports gear. It is easy to get good deals on branded shoes, outdoor clothes and gym wear. Other than all of these, there are various shops where you can get good deals on fashionable clothes. There are some factory outlets between Alexandra Parade and Johnston Street.

MELBOURNE TRAVEL GUIDE

You will find everything from accessories to jewelry here. You can reach Smith Street by catching tram number 86 from the city. It runs from 5am in the morning till midnight.

Bridge Road, Richmond

Melbourne, Victoria 3121

http://www.bridgerd.com.au/

Bridge Road is an established discount shopping area in Melbourne and is immensely popular with both locals and tourists. Along with several stores selling clothes, accessories and shoes at sale prices, the shopping area also offers great bars and cafés. Bridge Road is home to fashion boutiques which offer personal customer service and quality pieces at attractive prices. There is also a

MELBOURNE TRAVEL GUIDE

wide range of stores offering home furnishings featuring both antiques traders and furniture designers. You can reach Bridge Road by taking tram numbers 48 or 75 from the city centre. There are also tram numbers 79 and 78 from St Kilda and South Yarra respectively.

Queen Victoria Market

513 Elizabeth St

Melbourne, Victoria 3000

03 9320 5822

http://www.qvm.com.au/

The Queen Victoria Market is the mecca of shopping in Melbourne. It represents much more than just a market to the residents of the city. It is an institution, a historical landmark and a great tourist attraction all rolled into one.

MELBOURNE TRAVEL GUIDE

The market has twice made its way to the final list for the Victorian Tourism Awards (2010 and 2011). Whether you buy baggage or clothing, you will get great items at low prices. The market is segmented into sections including the Deli Hall, Fruit and Vegetables, General Merchandise, Elizabeth Street Shops, Vic Market Place Food Court, The Meat Hall, Victoria Street Shops, The Wine Market and Organics.

You can reach the Queen Victoria market by catching any tram which goes to William Street. It remains closed on Mondays and Wednesdays.

MELBOURNE TRAVEL GUIDE

Melbourne Central

211 Latrobe St

Melbourne, Victoria 3000

03 9922 1123

http://www.melbournecentral.com.au/

Melbourne Central is a modern shopping centre spread across several levels. The shopping centre boasts major brands as well as food and entertainment centres.

It is also famous for a giant pocket watch which makes all aware of its presence every hour. The shopping centre offers a wide range of choices in terms of food, culture, entertainment and fashion. There are several stores showcasing both international and Australian designers. The centre boasts more than 300 stores and has

MELBOURNE TRAVEL GUIDE

something to offer to both window shoppers and shopaholics alike.

Getting to the shopping centre is quite easy because it is located in the central business district of Melbourne You can catch the free tram service or any tram from St Kilda Road to Swanston Street to stop number eight.

Melbourne Central remains open from Monday to Saturday from 10 am to 6 pm with the exception of Friday when it is open till 9 pm. It remains open from 10 am to 3 pm on Sundays.

Bourke Street, CBD

231 Victoria Road, Fairfield

Melbourne, Victoria 3078

MELBOURNE TRAVEL GUIDE

Australia

+61 3 9489 8884

http://www.bourkestreet.com.au/

Bourke Street is the entertainment hub of Melbourne and is viewed as the second most important street in the city. It is great for both budget shoppers and also for visitors with money to splurge. The street is bustling with activity and boasts a huge range of stores, cafes and restaurants. Take a walk down some of the nearby streets and you will find good deals in the small and independent stores. The GPO building located nearby has some tasty treats awaiting you after you are finished shopping.

The street is open only to shoppers and trams so always listen out for the tram bells before walking from one store

MELBOURNE TRAVEL GUIDE

to another. You will find everything from beauty products to fashionable handbags all at the same place. There is also the **Bourke Street Mall** located nearby for some more shopping.

You can take tram 86, 95 or 96 to reach Bourke Street and it remains open everyday from 10 am to 10 pm.

Know Before You Go

 Entry Requirements

With the exception of New Zealand, nationals of most countries will need a valid passport and a visa when travelling to Australia. Upon arrival, you will also be required to fill out a passenger card, which includes a declaration regarding your health and character. A tourist visa is usually valid for 6 months, but can be extended for another 6 months. If travelling to Australia for business reasons, you will want to look into the requirements for a short term or long term business visas. The former is valid for up to 3 months, while the latter is valid for up to 4 years, but requires sponsorship from an Australian company.

Health Insurance

If visiting Australia from a country that has a reciprocal health care agreement with Australia, you will be able to use Medicare - Australia's public health insurance - for the duration of your stay. Participating countries include Ireland, New Zealand, Italy, Sweden, Norway, Slovenia, Belgium, Finland, the

MELBOURNE TRAVEL GUIDE

Netherlands and the UK. However, this only covers emergency care and limits you to using public hospitals. Visitors on a student visa from Norway, Finland, Malta and the Republic of Ireland may require additional cover and visitors who do not have access to Medicare will be required, as part of their visa application, to obtain adequate healthcare for the duration of their stay in Australia. To extend your cover, Overseas Visitors Health Cover (OVHC) can be arranged through a number of Australian health fund companies. Additional health insurance is mandatory if visiting on a long stay working visa. There are no required vaccinations for entering Australia, but a booster shot for tetanus and diphtheria will be a good idea, if your last vaccination was more than ten years ago. If travelling from Southeast Asia, you may want to get a shot for Hepatitis A and B, as well as typhoid.

Travelling with Pets

Nearly all dogs and cats travelling to Australia will need to spend some time in quarantine, but the duration depends on the country of origin. The only countries exempt from this requirement is New Zealand, Cocos Island and Norfolk Island. The minimum quarantine period is 10 days and to qualify for this, your pet will need to be tested for rabies 6 months prior to

MELBOURNE TRAVEL GUIDE

your travel date. The cost for quarantine and customs clearance is approximately $1,800AUD. You will need to apply for an import permit for your pet. If travelling from a non-approved country such as Russia, India, Sri Lanka and the Philippines, your pet will need to spend 6 months in an approved country and be tested for rabies prior to being allowed entry in Australia. Approved countries include Antigua & Barbuda, Argentina, Austria, the Bahamas, Belgium, Bermuda, the British Virgin Islands, Brunei, Bulgaria, Canada, the Canary and Balearic Islands, the Cayman Islands, Chile, the Republic of Croatia, the Republic of Cyprus, the Czech Republic, Denmark, Finland, France, Germany, Gibraltar, Greece, Greenland, Guernsey, Hong Kong, Hungary, Ireland, the Isle of Man, Israel, Italy, Jamaica, Jersey, Kuwait, Latvia, Lithuania, Luxembourg, Macau, Malta, parts of Malaysia (Peninsular, Sabah and Sarawak only), Monaco, Montenegro, the Netherlands, Netherlands—Antilles & Aruba, Norway, Poland, Portugal, Puerto Rico, Qatar, Reunion, Saipan, Serbia, Seychelles, Slovakia, Slovenia, South Africa, South Korea, Spain, St Kitts and Nevis, St Lucia, St Vincent & the Grenadines, Sweden, Switzerland (including Liechtenstein), Taiwan, Trinidad and Tobago, the United Arab Emirates, the United Kingdom, the United States, Northern Mariana Islands, Puerto Rico and the US Virgin Islands as well as American Samoa, Bahrain, Barbados, Christmas Island, Cook Island, the

MELBOURNE TRAVEL GUIDE

Falkland Islands, the Federated States of Micronesia, Fiji, French Polynesia, Guam, Hawaii, Iceland, Japan, Kiribati Mauritius, Nauru, New Caledonia, Niue, Palau, Papua New Guinea, Samoa, Singapore, the Solomon Islands, the Kingdom of Tonga, Tuvalu, Vanuatu and the Futuna Islands. There are quarantine stations in Sydney and Melbourne. A quarantine period can be waived in the case of service dog, provided that proper documented evidence of the dog's status is submitted, but in this case, the dog will need to be inspected upon arrival by an approved veterinarian and supervised for the 10 day period immediately after entry. You are not allowed to bring certain dog breeds such as the Dogo Argentino, Fila Brazileiro, Japanese Tosa, Pit Bull Terrier, American Pit Bull, Perro de Presa Canario or Presa Canario into Australia. Other animals that cannot be brought into Australia are chinchillas, fish, ferrets, guinea pigs, hamsters, lizards, mice, snakes, spiders and turtles. In the case of avian species, only birds originating from New Zealand are allowed.

Airports

Sydney Airport (SYD) is located just 8km south of Sydney's central business district and serves as the primary gateway for international air traffic into Australia. It is the country's busiest

MELBOURNE TRAVEL GUIDE

airport and provides connections to New Zealand, Singapore, Hong Kong, Dubai, Japan, the USA and Malaysia. Domestically, it also provides access to the country's six main states, as well as to Tasmania. The second busiest airport is **Melbourne Airport** (MEL). It is located about 23km from the central business area of Melbourne, but this is easy to reach via the Skybus Super Shuttle, which connects to the city's public transport network at the Southern Cross station. Melbourne Airport welcomes international flights from the Far East, the Middle East and the USA and also connects to Australia's top domestic destinations. The busiest airport in Queensland is **Brisbane Airport** (BNE), which provides connections to over 40 domestic destinations and over 25 international destinations. Other important airports in Queensland are the **Gold Coast Airport** (OOL) and the **Cairns Airport** (CNS). As the 4th busiest airport, **Perth Airport** (PER) serves as a gateway to Western Australia. **Adelaide Airport** (ADL) is the most important airport in the Southern Territory of Australia, while **Darwin Airport** (DRW), one of the oldest airports in Australia, opens up the Northern Territory. **Canberra Airport** (CBR) provides access to the capital. Tasmania is served by **Hobart International Airport** (HBA) in Hobart.

MELBOURNE TRAVEL GUIDE

🌏 Airlines

Qantas Airways is the third oldest airline in the world. It was founded in 1920 through the efforts of two Australian Flying Corps veterans, W Hudson Fysh and Paul McGinness. The enterprise pioneered a series of milestones, starting with the establishment of an airmail service, the Flying Doctor Service, a regular connection between Brisbane and Darwin and the addition of international destinations such as Singapore. Qantas was an early adapter to the benefits of Boeing jumbo jets and one of the first airlines to establish a trans-Pacific route. Today it is Australia's national flag carrier and the country's largest airline. Qantas is a partner of the OneWorld Air Alliance, connecting it with British Airlines, Iberia, Japan Airlines, Finnair, LAN Airlines and Sri Lankan Airlines.

Qantas has a founding interest in Australia's budget service, Jetstar Airways, which is based at Melbourne Airport. Together with Qantas, Jetstar oversees Jetstar Asia Airways, Jetstar Pacific Airlines and Jetstar Japan. Qantas also operates a regional brand, QantasLink, which harnesses the combined coverage of Eastern Australian Airlines, Sunstate Airlines and Southern Australia Airlines to provide a regional and domestic service. Eastern Australia Airlines was founded late in the 1940s, when it served mainly to connect remote rural

MELBOURNE TRAVEL GUIDE

communities under the name Tamair. During the mid-1980s, it was acquired by Australian Airlines, who in turn sold it to Qantas in 1992.

After Qantas, Virgin Australia is the second largest airline. Founded under the Virgin brand by Richard Branson and Brett Godfrey in 2000, the company expanded rapidly after September 2001 to fill the gap left by the demise of Ansett Australia. Virgin Australia is in partnership with the regional service SkyWest Airlines as well as Air New Zealand and the US carrier Delta. Additionally, it operates the budget airline, Tigerair Australia as a subsidiary of Virgin Australia. Tigerair offers connections to 11 domestic destinations as well as nearby Bali.

West Wing Aviation is a domestic service based in Queensland and manages connections to smaller and more remote destinations within Queensland. Airnorth was founded in the late 1970s. Based in Darwin, it provides a regional service that covers the northern part of Australia. King Island Airlines offers connections between Moorabbin, near Melbourne and King Island, Tasmania.

MELBOURNE TRAVEL GUIDE

🌐 Hubs

Sydney Airport serves as the primary hub for Qantas Air. Qantas also uses Melbourne Airport, Brisbane Airport, Perth Airport and Adelaide Airport as hubs. Virgin Australia uses Brisbane Airport, Melbourne Airport and Sydney Airport as hubs, but also has a strong presence at Adelaide Airport, Perth Airport and Gold Coast Airport. Additionally, Melbourne Airport serves as hub for the Virgin subsidiary Tigerair, as well as Jetstar Airlines. Darwin International Airport serves as a primary hub for Airnorth. West Wing Aviation uses Townsville Airport in Queensland as hub. Brisbane Airport serves as a hub for Sunstate Airlines.

🌐 Money Matters
🌐 Currency

The currency of Australia is the Australian dollar. Notes are issued in denominations of $5, $10, $20, $50 and $100. Coins are issued in denominations of 5 cents, 10 cents, 20 cents and 50 cents as well as $1 and $2.

MELBOURNE TRAVEL GUIDE

🌐 Banking/ATMs

ATM machines are widely distributed across Australia in both urban and rural locations. Besides bank lobbies, they are often found in shopping centers, service stations, convenience stores and pubs. You should be able to use bank cards that are part of the Cirrus, Plus or Maestro networks. Most ATMs will explicitly indicate which cards are accepted. Using a debit card is fairly easy in Australia, but many ATMs will charge an additional fee of $2 or more for non-customers. There are exceptions. As the Westpac banking group is partnered with several overseas banks including Bank of America, Scotia Bank and Barclays, customers of those banks will be exempted from the banking fee. An alternative to using your bank card is the Travelex Cash Passport, an easy-to-use prepaid card which can be topped up using your debit card.

🌐 Credit Cards

MasterCard and Visa are widely accepted throughout Australia, while Diners Club and American Express will also be legal tender at larger shops and chain stores. Some shops will decline credit cards for purchases under AUS$15 and surcharges may apply for some businesses. Until recently, credit card users in

Australia had the choice of using a PIN or signature as security for credit card transactions, but from August 2016, PIN-enabled cards will be mandatory. You should make sure that your credit card is compatible with this new policy. Also remember to advise your bank or credit card of your travel plans prior to your departure.

Tourist Tax

From July 2016, working backpackers will be taxed at 32.5 percent on their Australian income.

Claiming Back VAT

Visitors to Australia can obtain a refund on purchases of at least $300, spent at a single business. Residents of the Australia's External Territories - the Norfolk Islands, Christmas Island and the Cocos (Keeling) Islands - also qualify for a refund from GST paid under the Tourist Refund Scheme (TRS). To obtain a refund, you must present valid documentation of your purchases in the form of a tax invoice or sales receipt at an international airport or seaport when departing Australia and this should happen within 60 days of making those purchases. You should keep the goods handy within your hand luggage, to have it available for inspection. To save time, download the TRS app where you can enter details electronically and use a specially dedicated shortcut queue to process your claim.

Tipping Policy

In Australia, restaurants are required by law to pay their waiting staff a working wage and tipping is not really expected, although the influence of tourism as well as American culture has influenced Australian attitudes in recent years. In high-end restaurants, roughly half of the diners might be expected to leave a tip and in big cities, it will be more common to tip. If service is good and you want to show your appreciation, 10 percent is regarded as fair and sufficient. It is not common practice to tip in hotels and in casinos, tipping is forbidden. In bars, it is accepted practice to tell the bartender to keep the change. The same applies to cab drivers.

MELBOURNE TRAVEL GUIDE

 Connectivity

Mobile Phones

Australia uses the GSM mobile network, which means that it should be compatible with phones from the UK or the European Union, but may be incompatible with phones from the USA and Canada. If you are able to use Australian networks, you will still face the high charges levied for international roaming. There is an alternative. If your phone is unlocked, you will be able to replace your own SIM card with an Australian SIM card for the duration of your stay.

Australia has 3 basic mobile networks - Telstra, Vodafone and Optus. Telstra offers the best coverage of Australia's rural and more remote locations, but is also one of the more expensive operators. If you plan to stick to urban locations, the coverage offered by Optus and Vodafone might be sufficient for your needs. Telstra sim cards are available at $2, with recharge packages starting at $20. Data only packages are priced at between $30 and $50. Optus sim cards begin at $2 for just the sim, with top-ups priced at between $10 and $50. Vodafone pre-paid sim cards begin at $1 for just the sim, with data packages priced at between $3 and $15. For a super budget option, consider the deals offered by the reseller Amaysim,

MELBOURNE TRAVEL GUIDE

which also offers the option to pay for top-ups online, via PayPal.

Dialling Code

The dialling code for Australia is +61.

Emergency Numbers

General emergency: 000

Text Emergency Relay Service: 106

MasterCard: 1800 120 113

Visa: 1800 450 346

General Information

Public Holidays

1 January: New Year's Day

26 January: Australia Day

March/April: Good Friday

March/April: Easter Monday

MELBOURNE TRAVEL GUIDE

25 April: Anzac Day

23 June: The Queen's Birthday

25 December: Christmas

26 December: Boxing Day

There are various holidays that are celebrated at state level or within certain religious communities.

🌍 Time Zones

The Australian continent is divided into three different time zones. The eastern states of Queensland, Victoria and New South Wales, as well as the Australian Capital Territory and Tasmania fall under Australian East Standard Time (AEST), which can be calculated as Greenwich Mean Time/Co-ordinated Universal Time (GMT/UTC) +10. Australian Central Standard Time (ACST) is used in the Northern Territory, South Australia and in the town of Broken Hill, which is found in the western part of New South Wales. Australian Central Standard Time can be calculated as Greenwich Mean Time/Co-ordinated Universal Time (GMT/UTC) +9 and a half hour. Western Australia uses Australian Western Standard time, which can be calculated as Greenwich Mean Time/Co-ordinated Universal Time (GMT/UTC) +8.

🌐 Daylight Savings Time

For Daylight Savings Time, clocks are set forward by one hour at 2am on the first Sunday in October and set back one hour at 3am on the first Sunday in April. Queensland, Western Australia and the Northern Territory do not observe Daylight Savings Time.

🌐 School Holidays

In Australia, the academic year runs from January to December. Generally, schools open towards the end of January or very early in February. There is a 2 to 3 week break from the end of March or early in April, a winter vacation in June/July and a 2 week spring break in September or October. The summer vacation is usually from mid December to the end of January. Exact dates are set by the state authority in question and may vary.

MELBOURNE TRAVEL GUIDE

🌏 Trading Hours

Trading hours are set at state rather than national level, but in most states there are little or no restrictions on hours. Generally, shopping hours in Australia are from 8am to 9pm on weekdays, 8am to 5.30pm on Saturdays and 9am to 6pm on Sundays. Most non-essential businesses will be closed on ANZAC Day, Good Friday and Christmas Day. In South Australia, trade on Sundays and Public Holidays are restricted to the hours between 11am and 5pm. In Queensland, most shopping centers close at 5pm, but will stay open for late trade on one day of the week. In Western Australia, large businesses and chain stores are restricted to trading between 9am and 5pm from Monday to Saturday and between 11am and 5pm on Sundays and Public Holidays.

🌏 Driving Policy

Australians drive on the left hand side of the road. In most states, you will be able to drive on a foreign licence, provided that it is valid and that an English translation (or International Driver's Licence) is available. The minimum driving age varies from 16 years and 6 months in the Northern Territory to 18 in Victoria, but in most states it is 17 years. The speed limit is

60km per hour for cities and urban areas, 50km per hour in suburban areas and 110km per hour on highways and rural roads. Laws regarding texting and the use of cell phones while driving vary, but in most states, a hands-free kit is required. Learner drivers or inexperienced drivers are not allowed to handle their phones at all while driving. The legal limit for drinking and driving is a Blood Alcohol Concentration (BAC) of 0.05%, but learner drivers and inexperienced drivers are not allowed to drink at all when driving.

Drinking Policy

In Australia, the minimum drinking age is 18. Children under the age of 18 are only allowed on licenced premises, if accompanied by a parent. Only businesses with a liquor licence are allowed to supply alcohol to the public and by law, they are required to ask customers and patrons for some form of identification. Local councils in Australia have the power to declare an area a dry zone, which means that no alcohol may be consumed there. The ban may relate to a particular event or can apply on an ongoing basis.

MELBOURNE TRAVEL GUIDE

Smoking Policy

In the early 1990s, Australia introduced legislation to restrict smoking in public places. Smoking is banned in restaurants, bars and licenced clubs, although there are designated smoking areas. Recently, the ban was widened to include smoking in vehicles with children under the age of 18. Smoking is also forbidden in outdoor play areas for children, at swimming pools, bus stops and railway stations. In New South Wales, you may not smoke within 4m of a building entrance and in Western Australia, smoking is prohibited in the patrolled areas of beaches. All tobacco products are required by law to carry health warnings.

Electricity

Electricity: 230 volts

Frequency: 50 Hz

Australia's electricity sockets are compatible with the Type I plugs, a plug that features three rectangular pins or prongs, arranged in a triangular shape, with two of the pins set at opposing angles to each other. They are similar to the plugs and sockets used in Fiji. If travelling from the USA or Canada, you will also need a power converter or transformer to convert the

MELBOURNE TRAVEL GUIDE

voltage from 230 to 110, to avoid damage to your appliances. The latest models of certain types of camcorders, cell phones and digital cameras are dual-voltage, which means that they were manufactured with a built in converter, but you will have to consult your electronics dealer about that.

🌐 Food & Drink

When they have the time for a hearty breakfast, Australians love a fry-up similar to the full English breakfast with eggs, bacon, sausage, mushroom and baked beans. Other popular breakfast options include porridge, cereal and milk or simply a slice of toast with vegemite - that is Australia's twist on good old Marmite. Technically, Australia lies in the Orient and a robust community of Asian immigrants has ensured the enduring popularity of Asian cuisine. Australia also sometimes offers exotic game, in the form of kangaroo, emu and crocodile steak. Adventurous diners will want to sample bush food, but it is not for the faint of heart. Bush tucker originated with the hunter-gatherer lifestyle of Australia's Aboriginal people and incorporates a variety of home-grown fruits and vegetables, as well as edible seeds and insects. One of the best known delicacies is the witchetty grub, which can be eaten raw or

MELBOURNE TRAVEL GUIDE

cooked. Other indigenous staples include bush yam, bush banana, conkleberries and wattle seeds.

In Australia, beer is serious business, complete with its own lingo of buzz phrases. Australians refer to a can as a "tinnie", a case of 24 cans as a "slab" and a bottle of beer as a "brownie" or, in the case of a long-necked bottle, as a "tally". While a short-necked bottle is called a "stubby", do not mistake it with a "Darwin stubby", the Northern Territory variety with a 2.25 litre capacity. Even glasses are divided into "pints", "schooners", "middys" or "pots", according to size, and you should say "My shout" to announce your intention to buy the next round.

The most popular beer brands in Australia are VB (Victoria Bitter) and Castlemaine's XXXX Gold and other beers worth sampling include Carlton Draught, Toohey's Extra Dry, Hahn Premium Light, Crown Lager, Pure Blonde and James Boag's Premium. In Queensland and New South Wales, Bundeberg beer is another favorite. Australia has a robust wine industry, of which the best known export is Penfolds Grange. Other well established wineries are Wolf Blass, Lindemans, Rosemount, Jacob's Creek, Yalumba, Berri Estates, Yellowglen and Hardy Wine Co. Tasmania produces top notch whiskies, such as the award-winning Sullivan's Cove and great cider, such as Red

MELBOURNE TRAVEL GUIDE

Sails, Lost Pippin and Pagan Cider. When it comes to soft drinks, Coca-Cola rules. Australia's taste for coffee has been influenced by the significant community of Italian immigrants. Visiting techno-geeks can try the newly launched Smartcup, an Australian invention which can be linked to a CafePay app and lets you pay for your daily brew online.

Useful Websites

http://www.australia.com/en

http://wikitravel.org/en/Australia

https://www.australianexplorer.com/

http://www.downundr.com/tips-and-tricks/top-ten-destinations

http://www.britz.com.au/

http://www.driveaustralia.com.au/suggested-routes/

http://ozyroadtripper.com.au/

http://australiaroadtrip.co.uk/

https://www.ozexperience.com/

CPSIA information can be obtained
at www.ICGtesting.com
Printed in the USA
LVOW04s1438310816
502661LV00044B/866/P